DATE DUE

The story of the Jews' suffering under the
Pharaohs and their flight from Egypt. The
author explains the first Passover and the
traditional ways of celebrating it. Includes
descriptions of Passover observances today.

B 9-209

Passover

A CROWELL HOLIDAY BOOK

Passover

BY NORMA SIMON

Illustrations by Symeon Shimin

THOMAS Y. CROWELL COMPANY • NEW YORK

CROWELL HOLIDAY BOOKS

Edited by Susan Bartlett Weber

St. Valentine's Day

Passover

Arbor Day

Flag Day

Mother's Day

Library of Congress Catalog Card No. 65-11644

1 2 3 4 5 6 7 8 9 10

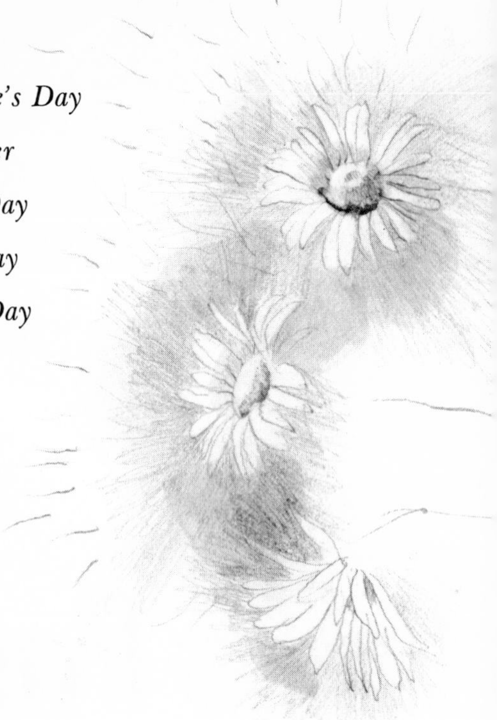

Passover

Early in spring, all around the world, Jewish families celebrate the holiday of Passover. With songs, poems, and prayers, with food and wine, the ancient story of Passover is told from father to son.

Passover begins with a special meal called the *Seder* and lasts for eight days. Each year, in each family, the Seder is the same. The children know that when they are grown and have their own families, they will make a Seder and teach their children the Passover story.

The story of the first Passover is written in the Old Testament in the Bible. It tells of the time three thousand years ago when the Jews left their homes in Canaan for the land of Egypt. There they tended flocks of sheep and lived in peace with the Egyptians. They spoke the Hebrew language and so were called Hebrews.

The Hebrews prayed to one God, even though the Egyptians prayed to many gods. The Pharaoh, who ruled Egypt, let them worship as they pleased.

When the Pharaoh died, a cruel new king came to power. He made the Hebrews slaves and forced them to build cities for him. For many years they carried heavy bricks, stones, and mortar and built great temples and pyramids.

The next Pharaoh was even more cruel. Soon the Hebrews lost almost all hope of becoming free men again. They cried out to God for help.

God chose a brave man, Moses, to lead the Hebrews out of slavery. He was not afraid of the Pharaoh. "Let my people go," he ordered.

The Bible tells of many miracles Moses performed to prove to the Pharaoh that he had come at God's command. But the Pharaoh refused to believe him.

So God sent plagues to Egypt. Hail fell from the skies and no crops could grow. The fish died in the rivers, and frogs, lice, locusts, and flies overran the land. But still the stubborn king refused to let the Hebrews leave.

The last plague was the worst of all. In every Egyptian house the eldest son died. The Hebrew sons were spared because Moses had told each family to sacrifice a lamb and rub the blood on the door of the house. The blood was a sign to God that a Hebrew lived there, so God's Angel of Death would *pass over* the house.

This is where the word "Passover" comes from.

On that first Passover night even the mighty Pharaoh lost a son. Saddened, he called Moses to him.

"Rise up, both ye and the children of Israel, and go," he said at last.

Moses quickly called the Jews together. There was no time to prepare food for the journey. They mixed wheat flour with water and carried the dough in wooden boxes on their shoulders with their other belongings.

When they reached the safety of the desert, they rested awhile. They baked the bread in the hot rays of the sun. The flat, unleavened bread, without yeast to make it rise, was called *matzah*.

The Pharaoh's sadness over the death of his son soon turned into anger. He ordered his soldiers to ride their chariots into the desert and capture Moses.

The Hebrews had reached the shore of the Red Sea when they saw the soldiers coming. The water was deep and there was no way to cross.

With God's help Moses performed another miracle. The waters of the Red Sea parted. The Hebrews walked safely through the sea to the opposite shore, but the Egyptians drowned as the water swept over them.

Then Moses led his people through the wilderness back to the land of Canaan.

Ever since that time the story of the Passover and the exodus from Egypt has been told over and over again. Some people believe it happened exactly as it is written in the Bible. Others believe that the story has changed in the telling, for it was not written down until one thousand years later. They call it a legend.

Men have studied the written records left by the Egyptians, hoping to learn more about Moses and the Passover. However, the Egyptians wrote very little about the Hebrews.

We know that a powerful Pharaoh ruled Egypt when a city called Pithom was built by the Hebrew slaves. The records also tell that the exodus was probably between 1300 and 1250 B.C.

Although the exodus was a small event in Egyptian history, it was a time of great rejoicing for the Hebrews. They were free men once again.

Each year they gave thanks to God for the Passover. In Canaan they prayed in a beautiful Temple built by King Solomon. Later, after the Temple was destroyed in a war, they worshiped wherever they could.

When at last the Temple was rebuilt, there was great excitement. Pilgrims came from all over the country and put up tents on the hillsides. Thousands of them in white holiday robes waited their turn to sacrifice the Passover lamb in the Temple. There were singing and music and prayers of thanksgiving.

The Hebrews always remained true to one God. Fathers taught their prayers, their customs, and their language to their sons. Even though many Hebrews left Canaan, or Israel as it was also called, to make new homes in other countries, they never forgot the Passover.

Today Jewish families live in nearly every country in the world. And for them spring always brings preparations for Passover.

During those eight days no other bread but matzah, the bread once baked in the desert, may be eaten. The day before the Seder the children and their father search the house. They make sure not even a tiny crumb of bread baked with yeast is left.

Some Jews have special dishes, glasses, silver, pots and pans for use only during the holiday. All other kitchenware is put away.

The mother buys sweet grape wine to drink at the Seder. She buys the meat, fish, and eggs for the Seder meal. And she buys packages of matzahs.

Not so long ago it was harder to get ready for Passover. Grandfathers fermented grapes and made the sweet wine themselves, as their fathers had done before them.

A week before the holiday, enough matzahs were baked for everyone in the town. The houses with the largest ovens were the bakeries and there were huge piles of the flat, unleavened squares.

Now, the afternoon before the Seder, the best tablecloth is put on the table. A bouquet of spring flowers and candles are placed on the table, too.

Polished silver, fine china plates, and a glass of wine are set at each place. The glasses will be filled and emptied four times during the Seder, so the children are given very small ones.

The largest wineglass on the table is called the Cup of Elijah. It is for the Biblical prophet Elijah, who is an invisible guest at the Seder. The children like to imagine that the prophet visits their Seder and drinks some of his wine. This is part of the legend of Passover.

Near the father's place is the *Matzah Cloth*. It may be made of plain linen or richly embroidered satin. It holds three matzahs. A large dish called the *Seder Plate* is placed on top of the cloth.

Fathers, mothers, grandfathers, grandmothers, aunts, uncles, friends, and children take their places at the Seder table. Tonight everyone at the table may sit as he wishes. Nobody has to sit straight in his chair. The father's chair is soft with cushions to remind everyone that he is a free man, no longer a slave to the Pharaoh.

Beside each place is a *Haggadah*, the Passover book. The Haggadah is a book of questions and answers. The children ask the questions and the father gives the answers. Like a play in which all the parts are written down, the Haggadah tells the story of the Passover and the order of the Seder.

Haggadahs are usually printed in Hebrew on the right side of the page and in English on the left side. Like all Hebrew books, the Haggadah begins at the place we call the back. The pages are then turned from left to right. Each person in the family reads from his own Haggadah.

The Seder begins with the blessing of the wine. Then the father breaks the middle matzah in his Matzah Cloth in two. He wraps the larger piece, called the *Afikoman*, in a napkin and hides it behind his cushions.

Then the youngest child stands and asks his father the important question, "Why is this night different from all other nights of the year?"

The father reads the answers to the question aloud from the Haggadah. As he tells of the bitterness of slavery under the Egyptians, everyone eats a piece of a bitter herb from the Seder Plate.

Everyone also tastes the *charoseth* from the Seder Plate. The charoseth is made of grated apples, nuts, cinnamon, and wine. It stands for the mortar used to hold together the bricks and stones of which the Pharaoh's cities were built.

The father tells of the terrible plagues the Egyptians suffered. Everyone spills a drop of wine for each plague.

Then he points to the roasted bone on the Seder Plate. It is a symbol of the lamb sacrificed at the first Passover.

When he repeats the story of Moses and the bread baked in the desert, everyone eats a piece of matzah.

On the Seder Plate, too, are a roasted egg and some parsley. The egg stands for the Seder feast that will follow, and the parsley for the new hope spring brings to the hearts of men.

Next the mother serves the Seder feast. The delicious food is eaten slowly, for no one may order a free man to hurry.

Then the father looks in the cushions of his chair. He is looking for the Afikoman, but the children have hidden it away. They giggle and the father pretends to be angry.

The children promise to return it if their father will give them a gift. He agrees very happily. Then he shares the matzah with everyone at the table, as the lamb was shared at Seders long ago.

The Seder ends with singing. The songs ring through the house as they once rang out in King Solomon's Temple. The children love the songs and know them by heart.

During the other days of Passover, the Songs of Solomon are read from the Bible. There are stories of last year's Seder and the children may beg their grandfather to tell about Passover when he was a boy. There is a mixture of memories in every family's Passover.

For Passover meals the mother cooks light, fluffy dumplings made of matzah-meal flour and eggs. She bakes soft, yellow sponge cakes. She fries matzah-meal pancakes which the children eat with sugar and jelly. For lunch there are often crisp matzah sandwiches.

While American families are sitting at the Seder table, far away in the country of Jordan a small group of Jews celebrates Passover in a different way. These are the Samaritans. They tend sheep in the grazing lands. The men have long beards and long hair.

On the eve of Passover, when the sun goes down, the Samaritans leave their homes. Dressed in snowy white robes, they lead their flocks of sheep past the square mud-brick houses and low trees which dot the countryside. When they reach the foot of nearby Mt. Gerizim, they set up their tents.

Then each family sacrifices a Passover lamb. The lambs are roasted in deep holes over the red coals of wood fires. By the time darkness covers the mountains, the meat is done.

The Samaritans eat the meat quickly, standing while they eat, as the Hebrews did during their flight from Egypt.

At the foot of the mountain under the stars they stand like ghosts of Moses and his people.

The Samaritans stay at Mt. Gerizim the eight days and nights of Passover. Their way of celebrating has always been the same.

Today in Israel, the homeland of the Jewish people, the first harvest of the year has been gathered by Passover. The growing time is all year round in this warm country. Red poppies and wild flowers from the fields decorate the homes.

Jerusalem, the capital city, is filled with Israeli pilgrims. Other Jews travel long distances to be with families and friends for the holiday.

Israeli citizens have come to their new country from many places. Often they escaped from war and persecution to the safety of Israel. The stories of their flights are told at Israeli Seders.

Before the Civil War in the United States, the story of Moses leading his people out of Egypt gave hope and comfort to the Negro slaves. They composed a song of freedom called "Go Down,

Moses." It uses the words Moses spoke
to the Pharaoh, "Let my people go."

Negro leaders were sometimes called
"Moses" by their followers. They led the
slaves to the North and freedom until
slavery was outlawed in all the states.

Slavery has been a part of the story of man since history began. Passover celebrates the Jews' escape from slavery and the right of men to be free. Each time Jewish children hear the story of Moses and the exodus they learn how important freedom is, not only for the Jews but for all mankind.

ABOUT THE AUTHOR

Norma Simon is particularly interested in the field of child guidance, and she has taught in nursery school, in kindergarten, and at the Vassar Institute for Family Living.

She received a B.A. in economics from Brooklyn College, and undertook graduate work in early-childhood education at the Bank Street College of Education and in psychology at the New School for Social Research.

Mrs. Simon enjoys a wide range of activities including cooking, gardening, modern dance, and folk music. She lives with her husband and three children in Norwalk, Connecticut.

ABOUT THE ILLUSTRATOR

Symeon Shimin was born in Astrakhan, on the Caspian Sea, in Russia, and came to the United States with his family ten years later. He attended art classes at Cooper Union in the evenings. Mr. Shimin painted for a while in the studio of George Luks, but he is primarily self-taught and found his schooling for the most part in the museums and art galleries in this country and in France and Spain.

In 1938, Mr. Shimin was chosen to paint a mural in the Department of Justice Building in Washington, D.C. Recognition and many invitations to museum exhibitions followed, including those at the Whitney Museum of Art, the Art Institute of Chicago, the National Gallery in Washington, D.C., and the National Gallery in Ottawa, Canada. His paintings are in public and private collections. In 1961, he held his first—and highly successful—one-man exhibition.